M000121207

THE
WINE LOVER'S
JOURNAL

whitecap

CONTENTS

An Introduction to Wine   5

Wineries Visited   31

Cellar Records   37

Tasting Notes   57

GRAND VIN

An Introduction
to Wine

APPELLATION
CONTROLEE

GRAND CRU CLASSE

e75 cl. 10.5% vol.

VISITING WINE COUNTRY

Wine is the product of its environment. The best way to learn about wine is to visit the place where it's made. It's amazing how your appreciation of a wine increases when you see the place it comes from. Wine also reflects the vintner's personality, so visiting a winery and meeting the winemaker can give you insight into the uniqueness of wines made there.

Visiting a winery is also excellent encouragement to start collecting wine. There's nothing like the opportunity to taste before you buy. Also, wineries always reserve specials lots or library wines that can be found only in their wine shops.

Many wineries offer experiences beyond tours and tastings. Many have outstanding on-site restaurants or catering facilities, which are often great places to eat—and good value.

The better prepared you are, the more you'll enjoy wine touring. Here are a few practical tips:

Be prepared. Have a good map that identifies winery locations.

Do some research. A good guidebook is invaluable. It never hurts to come armed with expert advice.

Time your visit to coincide with special events in the region, such as wine festivals or special winery functions.

Be open-minded. The glory of wine is its diversity. There's always something new to be discovered.

THE NORTH AMERICAN VINTNER'S YEAR

In the Vineyards

JANUARY   Vines are pruned.

FEBRUARY   Pruning continues; cuttings are placed in greenhouses.

MARCH   Soil is aerated by plowing around the base of the vines. Vines begin to come out of their winter dormancy.

APRIL   Cuttings are grafted onto rootstock to replace damaged vines. More plowing.

MAY   Flower buds open, despite the threat of late frosts. Vine suckers are pruned.

JUNE   Leaves and flower clusters develop; shoots and clusters are pruned; shoots tied to wires.

JULY   Grapes begin to develop. If conditions demand it, vines are sprayed to protect against mildew and fungi. Shoots are trimmed.

AUGUST   Grapes begin to ripen, sugar levels increase, acidity decreases and bulk increases. Vineyards weeded and vines trimmed.

SEPTEMBER   Acids continue to decrease; sugar continues to increase. Grapes are ready when sugar levels stop rising (approximately 40–45 days altogether). Grapes are harvested.

OCTOBER   Harvest continues. Compost and fertilizer spread on the vines.

NOVEMBER   Bases of vines are covered for protection; soil is aerated.

DECEMBER   Shoots are trimmed.

In the Cellar

JANUARY   Wines from previous vintages, now in barrels, are carefully maintained. Barrels are regularly topped up. Labelling and packing boxes of bottled wine for shipment is often done.

FEBRUARY   New wine from previous vintage is "racked off" into clean barrels to help it clear. The wine is often "assembled" in one or two large vats first to eliminate variations between individual barrels.

MARCH   Racking must finish before month's end. Some secondary fermentation occurs around the beginning of spring. Barrels must be continuously topped off to avoid "ullage" (empty space) in casks. Aromatic wines, fermented in stainless steel, are now ready for bottling.

APRIL   Topping-off is still performed. About five per cent of wine aged in traditional wooden barrels is lost to evaporation each year it spends in the wood.

MAY   Just before the vines flower, a second racking of the previous vintage is done to take the wine off its lees (sediment).

JUNE   Racking continues, finishing the new wine and racking off all wines in barrel storage in the cellar. Warm weather makes cask maintenance a doubly important chore.

JULY   All efforts are devoted to maintaining a cool constant cellar temperature. Some bottling is done.

AUGUST   Inspections are conducted, as well as cleaning and maintenance of vats, tanks and barrels to be used in the upcoming vintage.

In the Cellar

SEPTEMBER
All working metal parts of tanks and presses are sterilized. The main cuverie or fermenting tank is thoroughly scoured. Any wooden vessels used in fermentation are filled with water to swell the wood.

OCTOBER
While the vintage continues and new wine begins fermenting, year-old wine gets a final racking and the barrels are moved to "second year" cellaring for storage.

NOVEMBER
Racking and "fining" or filtering of wine ready to be bottled. Bottling is the big job. Lusty new wine is often ready to be racked first, toward the end of the month.

DECEMBER
Constant topping up of casks begins. Bottling, labelling and packaging of older wine continues.

HOW TO TASTE WINES

Start with a proper wine glass. Tulip-shaped ones are best for tasting. Be careful not to overfill your glass. For wine tasting, less is more. Before you taste, look. Hold the glass by the stem, and tilt it away from you, preferably against a white background, to examine the wine's colour. Remember that white wines darken as they age and red wines become paler.

Swirl the wine in the glass so that the sides get coated with wine. This is the moment of truth. Wine tasting is all about smell.

Sniff the wine gently. If you are patient, you will detect a progression of aromas. Try to identify the predominate smells.

Taste the wine. Take a small sip and swish it around in your mouth. Try to assess the balance between acidity, sweetness, astringency and bitterness. Spit out the wine and take note of the lingering aftertaste. The best wines always have clean, long-lasting flavours.

It can be challenging at first to find the right words to identify wine aromas. It's worth the effort so that, with a little practice, you can expand your wine vocabulary. At first, wine just tastes like wine. Each time you taste, you'll have more points of reference and your ability to enjoy wine will constantly expand.

THE AROMA WHEEL

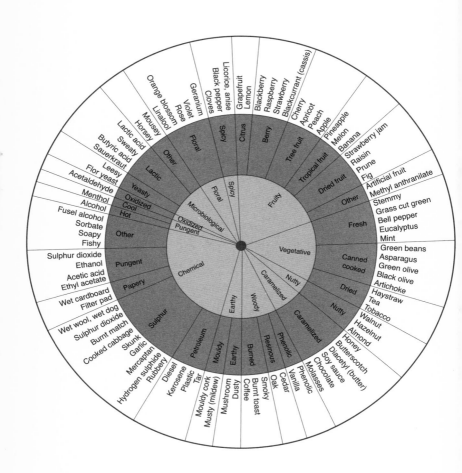

Devised at the University of California at Davis by Ann C. Noble, et al.

EVALUATING WINES

It pays to be diligent. You'll find that taking notes greatly enhances your enjoyment of wine. These are the basic qualities to comment on:

Date Tasted:

Name of Wine:

Occasion:

Food Eaten with Wine:

Guests:

Producer/Vintner:

Vintage:

Region: *Some labels tell you the region or village of the winery.*

Grape(s): *The variety of grape(s) is often noted on the label.*

Price:

Appearance: *Note colour, clarity, viscosity, depth of colour, etc.*

Bouquet: *The smell of the wine, often complex and referring to more than aroma.*

Taste: *Note sweetness, tannin, acidity and finish.*

Body & Balance: *Body refers to the weight or fullness of a wine, and balance refers to a wine's alcoholic strength, acidity, residual sugar and tannins.*

Comments: *Refer to the journal section "Tasting Notes" to record the wines you've sampled and your impressions.*

BUYING WINE

Reading Wine Labels

THE NEW WORLD
Wine labels from North and South America, Australia
and South Africa are almost always easy to understand.
Wines from these countries are labelled and marketed by
grape variety, which appears on the label second only in
prominence to the name of the winery. The vintage year
and/or geographical area may be specified in smaller
type under the grape variety. For example, a California
Chardonnay label will read:

Grand Ridge
CHARDONNAY
Napa Valley
(vintage)

Most "New World" wine labels follow this pattern with
slight variations. European countries, however, have
wine regulation and naming systems that have evolved
over centuries and give prominence to geographical area
rather than grape variety. In recent years, European
wine producers have begun designing labels to more
prominently display the grape variety, in response to
international market pressure. For example, a generic
red Burgundy, which used to be labelled "Vin de
Bourgogne," will now proclaim itself "Pinot Noir."

FRANCE
The *Appellation d'Origine Contrôlée* (AOC) is the primary
system of regulating wine in France. It grants producers
the right to use a "controlled name" as a guarantee of
geographical origin, grape varieties used and quantity
of wine produced from a specific area. Approximately
one third of all French wines qualify for the AOC. Wines
that don't qualify may be labelled VDQS (*Vins Délimités de
Qualité Superieure*) or *Vins de Pays*. These latter categories
are where real bargains and unique specialty wines can
often be found.

A SAMPLE WINE LABEL
FROM RHEINPFALZ, GERMANY

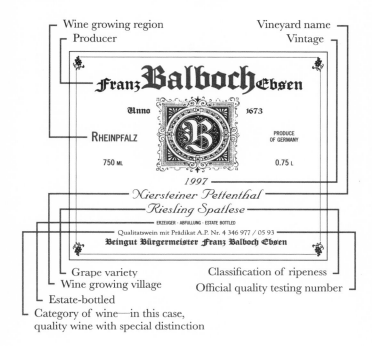

Wine growing region
Producer
Vineyard name
Vintage

Franz **Balboch** Ebsen

Anno   1673

RHEINPFALZ

PRODUCE OF GERMANY

750 ML   0.75 L

1997

Niersteiner Pettenthal

Riesling Spatlese

ERZEUGER · ABFULLUNG · ESTATE BOTTLED

Qualitatswein mit Prädikat A.P. Nr. 4 346 977 / 05 93

Weingut Bürgermeister Franz Balboch Ebsen

Grape variety
Wine growing village
Estate-bottled
Category of wine—in this case,
quality wine with special distinction

Classification of ripeness
Official quality testing number

A SAMPLE WINE LABEL
FROM BORDEAUX, FRANCE

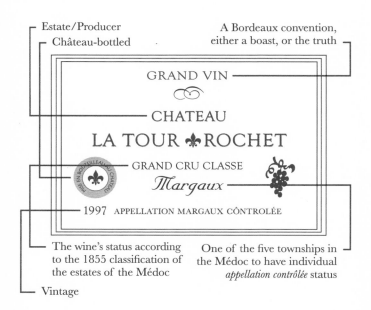

Estate/Producer
Château-bottled
A Bordeaux convention,
either a boast, or the truth

GRAND VIN

CHATEAU

LA TOUR ✦ ROCHET

GRAND CRU CLASSE

Margaux

1997   APPELLATION MARGAUX CÔNTROLÉE

The wine's status according
to the 1855 classification of
the estates of the Médoc

One of the five townships in
the Médoc to have individual
appellation contrôlée status

Vintage

ITALY

The designation of *Denominazione di Origine Controllata* (DOC) was introduced in the mid-20th century as the Italian answer to the French AOC. The designation *Denominazione di Origine Controllata e Garantita* (DOCG) denotes the highest quality level in Italian wine. *Vino da Tavola* (VdT) is the designation for everyday wines of unspecified origin. Since Italy has an overwhelming number of appellations and grape varieties, the first guide to quality is usually the producer's name.

GERMANY

German wine labels are the simplest to read. Dry wines and simple wines for everyday drinking are labelled *tafelwein* (table wine). The labelling of top quality wine is based on the amount of sugar contained in the grapes at harvest. Quality levels in *ascending* order of concentration, sweetness, rarity and price are as follows: Kabinett, Spätlese, Auslese, Beerenauslese, Trockenbeerenauslese and finally Icewein.

SPAIN

As in France and Italy, the labelling of Spanish wine focuses on the geographical area of origin. *Denominación de Origen* (DO) denotes wine from a quality-controlled wine region. Everyday country wines are labelled *Vino de la Tierra* (similar to the French VDQS).

A GENERAL NOTE

The term *"reserva"* on Spanish reds indicates, as do variant spellings in Italy and in South America, wines that have been set aside for extra aging in oak. Reserva/riserva wines may carry very similar labels to the basic "house" version of the wine and even come from the same vintage, but are slightly more expensive, reflecting their greater complexity and aging achieved through being kept in a barrel for a longer period.

Grape Varieties

WHITE VARIETIES

Chardonnay   Chardonnay is the world's most popular white wine grape. It's very adaptable and can be grown all over the world. It is capable of producing wines that have great complexity and longevity. Chardonnay typically displays green apple, tropical fruit, buttery, nutty, mineral aromas and flavours.

Chenin Blanc   Originally from France's Loire Valley, where it produces phenomenally long-lived wines, Chenin Blanc is also widely planted in South Africa, where it's called "Steen." It exhibits melon, apple, citrus and honey aromas.

Gewürztraminer   This is the easiest grape to identify. It's very aromatic, with a distinctive spicy, sometimes smoky aroma.

Muscat   The oldest cultivated grape. Muscat is very versatile, and wines made with it can be light and bone-dry or profoundly sweet. It has unforgettable exotic floral, grapey aromas.

Pinot Blanc   Once a secondary grape in Burgundy and an Italian workhorse, Pinot Blanc is growing in popularity. This grape can produce complex wines that combine earthiness and peachy/appley fruit.

Pinot Gris   Originally from Alsace but common in Northern Italy where it's called Pinot Grigio, this is an early ripening grape variety. Wines made from Pinot Gris grapes can be very rich in body and will have peach, pear and honeyed aromas.

8

Riesling	From Germany. Riesling wines are becoming more fashionable. They're extremely versatile, with a superb balance of fruit and acidity. Look for apple, apricot, peach and pear, often joined together with pungent earthy/diesel aromas.
Sauvignon Blanc	From the Loire and Bordeaux, Sauvignon Blanc is usually quite tart, and displays distinctive herbal/vegetal and earthy aromas. There will be hints of Granny Smith apple, and it will be grassy and herbaceous
Semillon	From Bordeaux, Semillon is a full-bodied grape. In Australia, Semillon produces intense, lemony dry wines. When affected by botrytis mold, it's used to produce the world's richest and most long-lived dessert wines.
Viognier	Once a rare Rhône Valley wine, Viognier is now expanding around the world. Interestingly, it's sometimes blended with Syrah to create intense, dark red wines. Viognier exhibits intensely aromatic, exotic honeysuckle and orange blossom aromas.

RED VARIETIES

Cabernet Franc	Native to the Loire Valley and Bordeaux, Cabernet Franc is increasingly popular. It has distinct green, earthy, herbal/vegetable aromas combined with black cherry and berry fruit.
Cabernet Sauvignon	The great grape of left-bank Bordeaux. Tiny berries produce inky, concentrated, intense long-lived wines. Aromas include black currant, cherry, plum, cedar, green pepper and tobacco.

Gamay	The grape of Beaujolais, Gamay is juicy, fleshy, soft and charming. The wine, a gorgeous pink-purple colour, exhibits "little red fruit" aromas of raspberry, strawberry, currant and cherry.
Grenache	The great grape of Châteauneuf du Pape in the southern Rhône Valley, Grenache is also very successful in South Australia. The grapes produce very ripe, rich, herbal wines with sweet plum and cherry aromas.
Malbec	The great red grape of Argentina, where it produces mellow and supple wines with full body and rich plummy fruit.
Merlot	The great grape of right-bank Bordeaux, Merlot is softer and rounder than Cabernet but is capable of equal greatness. It has rich, ripe, concentrated plum, cherry and berry fruit aromas and can also be intensely floral.
Nebbiolo	From Piedmont in Northern Italy where it produces powerful, tannic, long-lived Barolos and Barbarescos, Nebbiolo has intense violet, leather, road tar and truffle aromas.
Pinot Noir	The red grape of Burgundy and Champagne, Pinot Noir tends to be both pale in colour and notoriously changeable, but no wine is capable of greater complexity of flavour or richer texture. Wines made with this grape exhibit strawberry, plum, cherry, earth, beetroot, gamey, mushroom aromas and flavours.

Pinotage	The signature grape of South Africa, Pinotage is a cross between Pinot Noir and Cinsault and produces very distinctive, highly aromatic wines with earthy, leathery undertones.
Sangiovese	The great red grape of Tuscany, Sangiovese combines high alcohol and acidity with ripe plummy, cherry fruit. Capable of great age.
Syrah (Shiraz)	Native to the Rhône Valley, Syrah is currently one of the most fashionable red varieties. The wines are very dark and have concentrated peppery, smoky, earthy, jammy fruit flavours and aromas. Syrah can be very tannic.
Tempranillo	The great red grape of Spain, Tempranillo thrives in hot, arid conditions. Wines made from these grapes can age very well. Look for plummy, earthy, leathery, sweet vanilla aromas and flavours.
Zinfandel	This thick-skinned California grape produces heady alcoholic wines that exhibit pronounced peppery, spicy notes.

BLENDED WINES

The world of wine is always changing. Grapes are always being planted in new places. They're also being combined in more and more creative blends, often including several different grape varieties. The idea is that the sum will be greater than its parts. Many of the most celebrated wines in the world are blends. Be adventurous—try them.

STORING & SERVING WINE

IDEAL TEMPERATURE
10–12°C (40–50°F)

BEST METHODS FOR LAYING DOWN
Choose a well-ventilated, dry room, free from light and
vibration, in the coolest part of your house. All wine
bottles should be stored lying on their side to keep the
corks from drying out. Make sure you can reach the
bottles you want without having to disturb the others.

More important than storing wine at the stated ideal
temperature, is a storage area with a constant temperature—wine is adversely affected by wild swings in
temperature. Be sure your wine is stored in an odour-
free environment because wine can also be damaged by
odours such as those from onions, paint, varnish and
cleaning supplies.

The Parts of a Wine Bottle

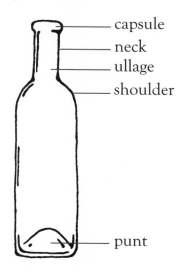

capsule
neck
ullage
shoulder

punt

Some Common Bottle Shapes

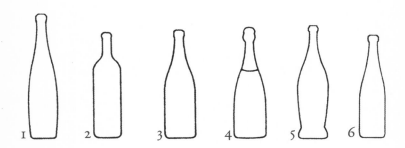

1. Alsace: The *flute d'Alsace* is usually slightly taller than German bottles, with a punt and green glass.

2. Bordeaux: Also called "claret" bottles, this is the classic shouldered bottle for red wines, with punt. Used worldwide. It may have to be stored lying on its side. These bottles come in dark green or pale green glass.

3. Burgundy: This is a slope-shouldered bottle, with a punt, used worldwide. The glass is medium to dark green for red and white wines.

4. Champagne: This bottle is slope-shouldered with a punt. Its glass is usually dark green and thicker than that used for still wines so that it can withstand the pressure. These types of bottles are used for most sparkling wines.

5. Côte de Provence: This is the traditional bottle for all Provence wines.

6. German Wine Bottle: Sometimes referred to as "hock" bottles, the bottles of Mosel wine are green, the others brown. The shape is similar to the *flute d'Alsace*.

A Sample Cellar

What's in your cellar will be dictated as much by budget and availability as by taste. Here's a sample collection that should give you enough variety to provide for any occasion. Ideally, you'll replace each bottle consumed with two bottles, and slowly build up your cellar.

Start with 48 bottles:

- 6 aperitif/sparkling: *Dry Sherry, Madeira, Sparkling Wine, Champagne*

- 6 everyday whites (under $15): *Riesling, Pinot Blanc, Sauvignon Blanc, Gewürztraminer, Chenin Blanc, Soave, Vinoho Verde*

- 6 everytday reds (under $15): *Merlot, Cabernet, Cabernet/Shiraz, Malbec, Côtes du Rhône, Valpolicella*

- 6 medium whites (under $25): *Chardonnay, Pinot Gris, White Rioja, New Zealand Sauvignon Blanc, Mediterranean Whites*

- 6 medium reds (under $25): *Pinot Noir, Red Rioja, Chianti, Côtes du Rhône, Merlot, Cabernet Sauvignon, Syrah/Shiraz*

- 6 big whites: *Burgundy, Loire, Top Alsatian and German Whites, Chardonnay, White Bordeaux, Semillon*

- 6 big reds: *Bordeaux, Burgundy, Châteauneuf du Pape, Chianti Riserva, Rioja Reserva, Zinfandel, Shiraz*

- 6 dessert: *Late Harvest, Icewine, Port, Liqueur Muscat, Vin Santo*

Serving Wine

DECANTING

Decanting is simply pouring wine from one container (the bottle it came in) into another.

There are two reasons to decant: to separate wine from sediment that has formed in the bottle over time, and for aeration. Young wine benefits from contact with air. It's helpful to decant young wine at least half an hour before drinking. Note that fine old wine shouldn't be decanted because its precious bouquet will dissipate very quickly.

GLASS SHAPES

Glasses should be clear and big enough that a serving fills only the bottom half of the glass. They should flare inwards to preserve the wine's aroma.

1. Champagne Flute: This glass is designed to prolong the wine's vivacity.
2. Brandy Snifter: Encourages warming of the brandy in the palm of the hand.
3. Baden Römer: For Rhine wine.
4. Port or Dock-Glass
5. Paris Goblet: Suitable for red wines when several wines are served.

6. I.N.A.O. (*Institut National des Appellations d'Origine*): Specially designed for tasting all wines and spirits.

7. Tulip: An all-purpose glass suitable for red and white wines or for whites when several wines are served.

8. Sherry Copita

9. Rhine and Mosel

OPENING AND SERVING

Invest in a good corkscrew that pushes down on the bottle at the same time as it draws the cork up and out. Open red wines an hour or so before serving. The host or hostess should pour a little wine into his or her own glass first to ensure that the guests don't get any crumbled cork that may have made its way into the bottle.

Fill each glass half full, then complete filling your own. A fresh glass for each new type of wine served is always a nice gesture but may not be practical, say, on a picnic in a kayak.

Champagne bottles should be opened by holding the bottle angled 45° away from you (to avoid damage to your eyes from flying corks). Hold the cork and turn the *bottle* until the cork comes away. Have a glass ready in case any precious drops of champagne come frothing out.

Wine & Food

Wine and food go together. In general, the rule "white wine with fish and red wine with meat" is a good guideline, but don't feel compelled to follow it slavishly. There are no rules. Personal taste matters more.

Wine lovers have always referred to the "marriage" of food and wine. Marriage can either be complementary or contrasting.

There are three key elements that combine to create the character of every wine, they are flavour, intensity and texture.

FLAVOUR
Successful food and wine pairings rely on either a similarity or a contrast of flavours. Serving a tart, crisp, high-acid Sauvignon Blanc with pungent, tangy goat's cheese is an example of similarity in flavour, while serving rich, sweet, vintage Port with sharp, tart Stilton cheese is an example of flavour contrast.

INTENSITY
The stronger the flavour of the wine, the stronger the flavour of the food should be. Mild, delicately flavoured Pinot Blanc paired with simple, pan-fried trout is an example of a low-intensity match. Pairing a bold, fruity Pinot Blanc with alder-grilled salmon with a mango, bell pepper and red onion salsa is a good example of a high-intensity match.

TEXTURE

The impact of the fruit, alcohol, acid and tannin in
the wine dictates its texture. Serving a rich, creamy
Chardonnay with scallops in a tarragon buerre blanc
will give similarity in texture, while serving a young,
firm Chardonnay with high acid alongside rich, creamy
Camembert cheese will show texture contrast.

If you're serving more than one wine with a meal, you
might find these guidelines helpful:

White before red

Young before old

Dry before sweet

Light before heavy

HOSTING A WINE-TASTING PARTY

Most wine tastings are wonderfully informal: a friend or
two, an interesting but unfamiliar bottle of wine, glasses
and a corkscrew.

You can host a more serious wine tasting at home,
which combines the best features of both the critical and
the convivial.

Sample a selection of no more than six similar wines,
ideally from the same vintage, region and grape variety. Comparing Cabernet Sauvignon against Shiraz or
Sangiovese is like comparing apples and oranges. Even
if you spit out the wine, the discriminatory powers of
taste buds deteriorate markedly after six sips, so you
might as well swallow and enjoy. If this is a co-operative
event (and it should be), every guest or couple could be
asked to bring a specific contribution for tasting. Make
sure that your directions as to the wine you want are
completely clear. Either six or twelve people is a good
number, since each bottle divides into six full glasses or
twelve "tasting-size" two-ounce samples.

Hold the tasting first—no drinking beforehand to blunt
the taste buds. You have the rest of the evening to relax
and imbibe uncritically.

If you have 12 guests and want to provide a fresh
glass for each of six wines, you'll need 72 glasses.
Alternatively, you can issue everyone a single glass and
provide facilities for rinsing it. This is the simplest way
to go, as long as you have plenty of clean, lint-free linen
napkins on hand to wipe down glasses and a carafe
of neutral distilled water to rinse the glasses and the
mouths of tasters between tastings.

If you have access to six decanters, decant the six cho-
sen wines half an hour before showtime, provided they
aren't the type that will expire before being tasted.

If you choose not to decant, a sheet of paper carefully taped around the bottle to hide the label will suffice. Just be careful to pick the bottle up by the shoulder and bottom while pouring, or it may slide out of the improvised sleeve with disastrous results. Number each sleeve with a felt pen so that no one gets confused about which wine they're drinking.

Provide tasting notes, photocopied from the journal (pages 57–127), for each guest and keep the journal to record this event for posterity.

Serve everyone the same wine at the same time, so you're all talking about the same subject, before moving to the next.

It's a good idea to provide bread to clear the palate between wines during the tasting phase. Save the feast for after.

At the end of the tasting, you may want to disclose the prices of each of the wines tasted and discuss which wines represent the best value.

After trying several comparative tastings, you may want to experiment with a "vertical" tasting. This is a tasting of different vintages of the same wine. As vintage wine can be expensive, it's a good idea to ask each person participating to provide a bottle. A vertical tasting allows you and your friends to compare notes on how a wine from a single house varies and changes with time.

Whatever style of wine tasting you try, above all, enjoy!

GRAND VIN

Wineries
Visited

APPELLATION
CONTROLEE

GRAND CRU CLASSE
e75 cl. 10.5% vol.

Date
_____

Name of Winery
_____

Location
_____

Grapes Grown
_____

Wines Produced
_____

Vintages Tasted
_____

Comments on Tastings
_____

_____

_____

Vintages Purchased
_____

Date
_____

Name of Winery
_____

Location
_____

Grapes Grown
_____

Wines Produced
_____

Vintages Tasted
_____

Comments on Tastings
_____

_____

_____

Vintages Purchased
_____

Date
_____

Name of Winery
_____

Location
_____

Grapes Grown
_____

Wines Produced
_____

Vintages Tasted
_____

Comments on Tastings
_____

_____

_____

Vintages Purchased
_____

_____

Date
_____

Name of Winery
_____

Location
_____

Grapes Grown
_____

Wines Produced
_____

Vintages Tasted
_____

Comments on Tastings
_____

_____

_____

Vintages Purchased
_____

_____

Date
_____

Name of Winery
_____

Location
_____

Grapes Grown
_____

Wines Produced
_____

Vintages Tasted
_____

Comments on Tastings
_____

_____

_____

Vintages Purchased
_____

Date
_____

Name of Winery
_____

Location
_____

Grapes Grown
_____

Wines Produced
_____

Vintages Tasted
_____

Comments on Tastings
_____

_____

_____

Vintages Purchased
_____

Date

Name of Winery

Location

Grapes Grown

Wines Produced

Vintages Tasted

Comments on Tastings

Vintages Purchased

Date

Name of Winery

Location

Grapes Grown

Wines Produced

Vintages Tasted

Comments on Tastings

Vintages Purchased

Date

Name of Winery

Location

Grapes Grown

Wines Produced

Vintages Tasted

Comments on Tastings

Vintages Purchased

Date

Name of Winery

Location

Grapes Grown

Wines Produced

Vintages Tasted

Comments on Tastings

Vintages Purchased

GRAND VIN

Cellar
Records

APPELLATION
CONTROLEE

GRAND CRU CLASSE
e75 cl. 10.5% vol.

Wine
_____

Vintage
_____

Region
_____

Producer/Shipper
_____

Grape Variety
_____

Place of Purchase
_____

Date Purchased
_____

Product Code
_____

Price
_____

Cellar Location
_____

Optimum Date for Consumption
_____

Comments
_____
_____
_____

GRAND RIDGE

Cabernet Sauvignon

2008
_____

CALIFORNIA
CANYON VINEYARDS

Paste your label here

Cellar Records | **The Wine Lover's Journal**

Wine

Vintage

Region

Producer/Shipper

Grape Variety

Place of Purchase

Date Purchased

Product Code

Price

Cellar Location

Optimum Date for Consumption

Comments

GRAND RIDGE

Cabernet Sauvignon

2008

CALIFORNIA
CANYON VINEYARDS

Paste your label here

Wine

Vintage

Region

Producer/Shipper

Grape Variety

Place of Purchase

Date Purchased

Product Code

Price

Cellar Location

Optimum Date for Consumption

Comments

GRAND RIDGE

Cabernet Sauvignon

2008

CALIFORNIA
CANYON VINEYARDS

Paste your label here

Wine
_____

Vintage
_____

Region
_____

Producer/Shipper
_____

Grape Variety
_____

Place of Purchase
_____

Date Purchased
_____

Product Code
_____

Price
_____

Cellar Location
_____

Optimum Date for Consumption
_____

Comments
_____
_____

GRAND RIDGE

Cabernet Sauvignon

2008

CALIFORNIA
CANYON VINEYARDS

Paste your label here

Wine

Vintage

Region

Producer/Shipper

Grape Variety

Place of Purchase

Date Purchased

Product Code

Price

Cellar Location

Optimum Date for Consumption

Comments

GRAND RIDGE

Cabernet Sauvignon

2008

CALIFORNIA
CANYON VINEYARDS

Paste your label here

Wine

Vintage

Region

Producer/Shipper

Grape Variety

Place of Purchase

Date Purchased

Product Code

Price

Cellar Location

Optimum Date for Consumption

Comments

GRAND RIDGE

Cabernet Sauvignon

2008

CALIFORNIA
CANYON VINEYARDS

Paste your label here

Wine

Vintage

Region

Producer/Shipper

Grape Variety

Place of Purchase

Date Purchased

Product Code

Price

Cellar Location

Optimum Date for Consumption

Comments

GRAND RIDGE

Cabernet Sauvignon

2008

CALIFORNIA
CANYON VINEYARDS

Paste your label here

Wine

Vintage

Region

Producer/Shipper

Grape Variety

Place of Purchase

Date Purchased

Product Code

Price

Cellar Location

Optimum Date for Consumption

Comments

GRAND RIDGE

Cabernet Sauvignon

2008

CALIFORNIA
CANYON VINEYARDS

Paste your label here

46

Wine

Vintage

Region

Producer/Shipper

Grape Variety

Place of Purchase

Date Purchased

Product Code

Price

Cellar Location

Optimum Date for Consumption

Comments

GRAND RIDGE

Cabernet Sauvignon

2008

CALIFORNIA
CANYON VINEYARDS

Paste your label here

Wine

Vintage

Region

Producer/Shipper

Grape Variety

Place of Purchase

Date Purchased

Product Code

Price

Cellar Location

Optimum Date for Consumption

Comments

GRAND RIDGE

Cabernet Sauvignon

2008

CALIFORNIA
CANYON VINEYARDS

Paste your label here

Wine
_____

Vintage
_____

Region
_____

Producer/Shipper
_____

Grape Variety
_____

Place of Purchase
_____

Date Purchased
_____

Product Code
_____

Price
_____

Cellar Location
_____

Optimum Date for Consumption
_____

Comments
_____

_____

GRAND RIDGE

Cabernet Sauvignon

2008

_____

CALIFORNIA
CANYON VINEYARDS

Paste your label here

Wine

Vintage

Region

Producer/Shipper

Grape Variety

Place of Purchase

Date Purchased

Product Code

Price

Cellar Location

Optimum Date for Consumption

Comments

GRAND RIDGE

Cabernet Sauvignon

2008

CALIFORNIA
CANYON VINEYARDS

Paste your label here

Wine
_____

Vintage
_____

Region
_____

Producer/Shipper
_____

Grape Variety
_____

Place of Purchase
_____

Date Purchased
_____

Product Code
_____

Price
_____

Cellar Location
_____

Optimum Date for Consumption
_____

Comments
_____
_____
_____

GRAND RIDGE

Cabernet Sauvignon

2008
_____

CALIFORNIA
CANYON VINEYARDS

Paste your label here

Wine

Vintage

Region

Producer/Shipper

Grape Variety

Place of Purchase

Date Purchased

Product Code

Price

Cellar Location

Optimum Date for Consumption

Comments

GRAND RIDGE

Cabernet Sauvignon

2008

CALIFORNIA
CANYON VINEYARDS

Paste your label here

Wine

Vintage

Region

Producer/Shipper

Grape Variety

Place of Purchase

Date Purchased

Product Code

Price

Cellar Location

Optimum Date for Consumption

Comments

GRAND RIDGE

Cabernet Sauvignon

2008

CALIFORNIA
CANYON VINEYARDS

Paste your label here

Wine

Vintage

Region

Producer/Shipper

Grape Variety

Place of Purchase

Date Purchased

Product Code

Price

Cellar Location

Optimum Date for Consumption

Comments

GRAND RIDGE

Cabernet Sauvignon

2008

CALIFORNIA
CANYON VINEYARDS

Paste your label here

Wine

Vintage

Region

Producer/Shipper

Grape Variety

Place of Purchase

Date Purchased

Product Code

Price

Cellar Location

Optimum Date for Consumption

Comments

GRAND RIDGE

Cabernet Sauvignon

2008

CALIFORNIA
CANYON VINEYARDS

Paste your label here

Wine

Vintage

Region

Producer/Shipper

Grape Variety

Place of Purchase

Date Purchased

Product Code

Price

Cellar Location

Optimum Date for Consumption

Comments

GRAND RIDGE

ᦞ

Cabernet Sauvignon

2008

CALIFORNIA
CANYON VINEYARDS

Paste your label here

Wine

Vintage

Region

Producer/Shipper

Grape Variety

Place of Purchase

Date Purchased

Product Code

Price

Cellar Location

Optimum Date for Consumption

Comments

GRAND RIDGE

Cabernet Sauvignon

2008

CALIFORNIA
CANYON VINEYARDS

Paste your label here

GRAND VIN

Tasting
Notes

APPELLATION
CONTROLEE

GRAND CRU CLASSE
e75 cl. 10.5% vol.

58

Date Tasted

Wine

Occasion

Food Eaten with Wine

Other Guests

Producer/Vintner

Vintage

Region

Grape(s)

Price   Product Code

Appearance   Bouquet

Taste   Body & Balance

Comments

GRAND RIDGE

Cabernet Sauvignon

2008

CALIFORNIA
CANYON VINEYARDS

Paste your label here

Tasting Notes | The Wine Lover's Journal

Date Tasted

Wine

Occasion

Food Eaten with Wine

Other Guests

Producer/Vintner

Vintage

Region

Grape(s)

Price   Product Code

Appearance   Bouquet

Taste   Body & Balance

Comments

GRAND RIDGE

Cabernet Sauvignon

2008

CALIFORNIA
CANYON VINEYARDS

Paste your label here

60

Date Tasted

Wine

Occasion

Food Eaten with Wine

Other Guests

Producer/Vintner

Vintage

Region

Grape(s)

Price   Product Code

Appearance   Bouquet

Taste   Body & Balance

Comments

GRAND RIDGE

Cabernet Sauvignon

2008

CALIFORNIA
CANYON VINEYARDS

Paste your label here

Date Tasted
_____

Wine
_____

Occasion
_____

Food Eaten with Wine
_____

Other Guests
_____

Producer/Vintner
_____

Vintage
_____

Region
_____

Grape(s)
_____

Price   Product Code
_____

Appearance   Bouquet
_____

Taste   Body & Balance
_____

Comments
_____

GRAND RIDGE

Cabernet Sauvignon

2008

CALIFORNIA
CANYON VINEYARDS

Paste your label here

Date Tasted
_____

Wine
_____

Occasion
_____

Food Eaten with Wine
_____

Other Guests
_____

Producer/Vintner
_____

Vintage
_____

Region
_____

Grape(s)
_____

Price	Product Code
Appearance	Bouquet
Taste	Body & Balance

Comments
_____

GRAND RIDGE

Cabernet Sauvignon

2008

CALIFORNIA
CANYON VINEYARDS

Paste your label here

Date Tasted

Wine

Occasion

Food Eaten with Wine

Other Guests

Producer/Vintner

Vintage

Region

Grape(s)

Price   Product Code

Appearance   Bouquet

Taste   Body & Balance

Comments

GRAND RIDGE

∞

Cabernet Sauvignon

2008

CALIFORNIA
CANYON VINEYARDS

Paste your label here

Date Tasted

Wine

Occasion

Food Eaten with Wine

Other Guests

Producer/Vintner

Vintage

Region

Grape(s)

Price   Product Code

Appearance   Bouquet

Taste   Body & Balance

Comments

GRAND RIDGE

Cabernet Sauvignon

2008

CALIFORNIA
CANYON VINEYARDS

Paste your label here

Date Tasted

Wine

Occasion

Food Eaten with Wine

Other Guests

Producer/Vintner

Vintage

Region

Grape(s)

Price   Product Code

Appearance   Bouquet

Taste   Body & Balance

Comments

GRAND RIDGE

Cabernet Sauvignon

2008

CALIFORNIA
CANYON VINEYARDS

Paste your label here

Date Tasted
_____

Wine
_____

Occasion
_____

Food Eaten with Wine
_____

Other Guests
_____

Producer/Vintner
_____

Vintage
_____

Region
_____

Grape(s)
_____

Price   Product Code
_____

Appearance   Bouquet
_____

Taste   Body & Balance
_____

Comments
_____

GRAND RIDGE

Cabernet Sauvignon

2008

CALIFORNIA
CANYON VINEYARDS

Paste your label here

Date Tasted

Wine

Occasion

Food Eaten with Wine

Other Guests

Producer/Vintner

Vintage

Region

Grape(s)

Price   Product Code

Appearance   Bouquet

Taste   Body & Balance

Comments

GRAND RIDGE

Cabernet Sauvignon

2008

CALIFORNIA
CANYON VINEYARDS

Paste your label here

Date Tasted
_____

Wine
_____

Occasion
_____

Food Eaten with Wine
_____

Other Guests
_____

Producer/Vintner
_____

Vintage
_____

Region
_____

Grape(s)
_____

Price   Product Code
_____

Appearance   Bouquet
_____

Taste   Body & Balance
_____

Comments
_____

GRAND RIDGE

Cabernet Sauvignon

2008

CALIFORNIA
CANYON VINEYARDS

Paste your label here

Date Tasted

Wine

Occasion

Food Eaten with Wine

Other Guests

Producer/Vintner

Vintage

Region

Grape(s)

Price   Product Code

Appearance   Bouquet

Taste   Body & Balance

Comments

GRAND RIDGE

Cabernet Sauvignon

2008

CALIFORNIA
CANYON VINEYARDS

Paste your label here

Date Tasted

Wine

Occasion

Food Eaten with Wine

Other Guests

Producer/Vintner

Vintage

Region

Grape(s)

Price   Product Code

Appearance   Bouquet

Taste   Body & Balance

Comments

GRAND RIDGE

Cabernet Sauvignon

2008

CALIFORNIA
CANYON VINEYARDS

Paste your label here

Date Tasted
_____

Wine
_____

Occasion
_____

Food Eaten with Wine
_____

Other Guests
_____

Producer/Vintner
_____

Vintage
_____

Region
_____

Grape(s)
_____

Price	Product Code

Appearance	Bouquet

Taste	Body & Balance

Comments
_____

GRAND RIDGE

Cabernet Sauvignon

2008

CALIFORNIA
CANYON VINEYARDS

Paste your label here

Date Tasted
_____

Wine
_____

Occasion
_____

Food Eaten with Wine
_____

Other Guests
_____

Producer/Vintner
_____

Vintage
_____

Region
_____

Grape(s)
_____

Price   Product Code
_____

Appearance   Bouquet
_____

Taste   Body & Balance
_____

Comments
_____

GRAND RIDGE

Cabernet Sauvignon

2008

CALIFORNIA
CANYON VINEYARDS

Paste your label here

Date Tasted

Wine

Occasion

Food Eaten with Wine

Other Guests

Producer/Vintner

Vintage

Region

Grape(s)

Price   Product Code

Appearance   Bouquet

Taste   Body & Balance

Comments

GRAND RIDGE

Cabernet Sauvignon

2008

CALIFORNIA
CANYON VINEYARDS

Paste your label here

Date Tasted
_____

Wine
_____

Occasion
_____

Food Eaten with Wine
_____

Other Guests
_____

Producer/Vintner
_____

Vintage
_____

Region
_____

Grape(s)
_____

Price	Product Code

Appearance	Bouquet

Taste	Body & Balance

Comments
_____

GRAND RIDGE

Cabernet Sauvignon

2008

CALIFORNIA
CANYON VINEYARDS

Paste your label here

Date Tasted

Wine

Occasion

Food Eaten with Wine

Other Guests

Producer/Vintner

Vintage

Region

Grape(s)

Price   Product Code

Appearance   Bouquet

Taste   Body & Balance

Comments

GRAND RIDGE

Cabernet Sauvignon

2008

CALIFORNIA
CANYON VINEYARDS

Paste your label here

Date Tasted

Wine

Occasion

Food Eaten with Wine

Other Guests

Producer/Vintner

Vintage

Region

Grape(s)

Price   Product Code

Appearance   Bouquet

Taste   Body & Balance

Comments

GRAND RIDGE

Cabernet Sauvignon

2008

CALIFORNIA
CANYON VINEYARDS

Paste your label here

Date Tasted

Wine

Occasion

Food Eaten with Wine

Other Guests

Producer/Vintner

Vintage

Region

Grape(s)

Price   Product Code

Appearance   Bouquet

Taste   Body & Balance

Comments

GRAND RIDGE

☙

Cabernet Sauvignon

2008

CALIFORNIA
CANYON VINEYARDS

Paste your label here

Date Tasted

Wine

Occasion

Food Eaten with Wine

Other Guests

Producer/Vintner

Vintage

Region

Grape(s)

Price	Product Code
Appearance	Bouquet
Taste	Body & Balance

Comments

GRAND RIDGE

Cabernet Sauvignon

2008

CALIFORNIA
CANYON VINEYARDS

Paste your label here

Date Tasted

Wine

Occasion

Food Eaten with Wine

Other Guests

Producer/Vintner

Vintage

Region

Grape(s)

Price   Product Code

Appearance   Bouquet

Taste   Body & Balance

Comments

GRAND RIDGE

Cabernet Sauvignon

2008

CALIFORNIA
CANYON VINEYARDS

Paste your label here

Date Tasted
_____

Wine
_____

Occasion
_____

Food Eaten with Wine
_____

Other Guests
_____

Producer/Vintner
_____

Vintage
_____

Region
_____

Grape(s)
_____

Price   Product Code
_____

Appearance   Bouquet
_____

Taste   Body & Balance
_____

Comments
_____

GRAND RIDGE

Cabernet Sauvignon

2008

CALIFORNIA
CANYON VINEYARDS

Paste your label here

Date Tasted

Wine

Occasion

Food Eaten with Wine

Other Guests

Producer/Vintner

Vintage

Region

Grape(s)

Price   Product Code

Appearance   Bouquet

Taste   Body & Balance

Comments

GRAND RIDGE

Cabernet Sauvignon

2008

CALIFORNIA
CANYON VINEYARDS

Paste your label here

Date Tasted

Wine

Occasion

Food Eaten with Wine

Other Guests

Producer/Vintner

Vintage

Region

Grape(s)

Price   Product Code

Appearance   Bouquet

Taste   Body & Balance

Comments

GRAND RIDGE

Cabernet Sauvignon

2008

CALIFORNIA
CANYON VINEYARDS

Paste your label here

Date Tasted

Wine

Occasion

Food Eaten with Wine

Other Guests

Producer/Vintner

Vintage

Region

Grape(s)

Price   Product Code

Appearance   Bouquet

Taste   Body & Balance

Comments

GRAND RIDGE

Cabernet Sauvignon

2008

CALIFORNIA
CANYON VINEYARDS

Paste your label here

Date Tasted

Wine

Occasion

Food Eaten with Wine

Other Guests

Producer/Vintner

Vintage

Region

Grape(s)

Price   Product Code

Appearance   Bouquet

Taste   Body & Balance

Comments

GRAND RIDGE

∞

Cabernet Sauvignon

2008

CALIFORNIA
CANYON VINEYARDS

Paste your label here

["

Date Tasted
_____

Wine
_____

Occasion
_____

Food Eaten with Wine
_____

Other Guests
_____

Producer/Vintner
_____

Vintage
_____

Region
_____

Grape(s)
_____

Price   Product Code
_____

Appearance   Bouquet
_____

Taste   Body & Balance
_____

Comments
_____

GRAND RIDGE

Cabernet Sauvignon

2008

CALIFORNIA
CANYON VINEYARDS

Paste your label here

Date Tasted
_____

Wine
_____

Occasion
_____

Food Eaten with Wine
_____

Other Guests
_____

Producer/Vintner
_____

Vintage
_____

Region
_____

Grape(s)
_____

Price   Product Code
_____

Appearance   Bouquet
_____

Taste   Body & Balance
_____

Comments
_____

GRAND RIDGE

Cabernet Sauvignon

2008

CALIFORNIA
CANYON VINEYARDS

Paste your label here

88

Date Tasted
_____

Wine
_____

Occasion
_____

Food Eaten with Wine
_____

Other Guests
_____

Producer/Vintner
_____

Vintage
_____

Region
_____

Grape(s)
_____

Price   Product Code
_____

Appearance   Bouquet
_____

Taste   Body & Balance
_____

Comments
_____

GRAND RIDGE

Cabernet Sauvignon

2008
———————————————

CALIFORNIA
CANYON VINEYARDS

Paste your label here

Date Tasted

Wine

Occasion

Food Eaten with Wine

Other Guests

Producer/Vintner

Vintage

Region

Grape(s)

Price   Product Code

Appearance   Bouquet

Taste   Body & Balance

Comments

GRAND RIDGE

Cabernet Sauvignon

2008

CALIFORNIA
CANYON VINEYARDS

Paste your label here

Date Tasted

Wine

Occasion

Food Eaten with Wine

Other Guests

Producer/Vintner

Vintage

Region

Grape(s)

Price   Product Code

Appearance   Bouquet

Taste   Body & Balance

Comments

GRAND RIDGE

Cabernet Sauvignon

2008

CALIFORNIA
CANYON VINEYARDS

Paste your label here

Date Tasted

Wine

Occasion

Food Eaten with Wine

Other Guests

Producer/Vintner

Vintage

Region

Grape(s)

Price   Product Code

Appearance   Bouquet

Taste   Body & Balance

Comments

GRAND RIDGE

Cabernet Sauvignon

2008

CALIFORNIA
CANYON VINEYARDS

Paste your label here

Date Tasted

Wine

Occasion

Food Eaten with Wine

Other Guests

Producer/Vintner

Vintage

Region

Grape(s)

Price   Product Code

Appearance   Bouquet

Taste   Body & Balance

Comments

GRAND RIDGE

Cabernet Sauvignon

2008

CALIFORNIA
CANYON VINEYARDS

Paste your label here

Date Tasted

Wine

Occasion

Food Eaten with Wine

Other Guests

Producer/Vintner

Vintage

Region

Grape(s)

Price   Product Code

Appearance   Bouquet

Taste   Body & Balance

Comments

GRAND RIDGE

Cabernet Sauvignon

2008

CALIFORNIA
CANYON VINEYARDS

Paste your label here

Date Tasted

Wine

Occasion

Food Eaten with Wine

Other Guests

Producer/Vintner

Vintage

Region

Grape(s)

Price   Product Code

Appearance   Bouquet

Taste   Body & Balance

Comments

GRAND RIDGE

Cabernet Sauvignon

2008

CALIFORNIA
CANYON VINEYARDS

Paste your label here

Date Tasted
_____

Wine
_____

Occasion
_____

Food Eaten with Wine
_____

Other Guests
_____

Producer/Vintner
_____

Vintage
_____

Region
_____

Grape(s)
_____

Price   Product Code
_____

Appearance   Bouquet
_____

Taste   Body & Balance
_____

Comments
_____

GRAND RIDGE

&

Cabernet Sauvignon

2008

CALIFORNIA
CANYON VINEYARDS

Paste your label here

Date Tasted
_____

Wine
_____

Occasion
_____

Food Eaten with Wine
_____

Other Guests
_____

Producer/Vintner
_____

Vintage
_____

Region
_____

Grape(s)
_____

Price _____ Product Code _____

Appearance _____ Bouquet _____

Taste _____ Body & Balance _____

Comments
_____
_____

GRAND RIDGE

∞

Cabernet Sauvignon

2008
_____

CALIFORNIA
CANYON VINEYARDS

Paste your label here

Date Tasted
_____

Wine
_____

Occasion
_____

Food Eaten with Wine
_____

Other Guests
_____

Producer/Vintner
_____

Vintage
_____

Region
_____

Grape(s)
_____

Price   Product Code
_____

Appearance   Bouquet
_____

Taste   Body & Balance
_____

Comments
_____

GRAND RIDGE

∽

Cabernet Sauvignon

2008

CALIFORNIA
CANYON VINEYARDS

Paste your label here

Date Tasted

Wine

Occasion

Food Eaten with Wine

Other Guests

Producer/Vintner

Vintage

Region

Grape(s)

Price   Product Code

Appearance   Bouquet

Taste   Body & Balance

Comments

GRAND RIDGE

☙

Cabernet Sauvignon

2008

CALIFORNIA
CANYON VINEYARDS

Paste your label here

Date Tasted

Wine

Occasion

Food Eaten with Wine

Other Guests

Producer/Vintner

Vintage

Region

Grape(s)

Price   Product Code

Appearance   Bouquet

Taste   Body & Balance

Comments

GRAND RIDGE

Cabernet Sauvignon

2008

CALIFORNIA
CANYON VINEYARDS

Paste your label here

Date Tasted
_____

Wine
_____

Occasion
_____

Food Eaten with Wine
_____

Other Guests
_____

Producer/Vintner
_____

Vintage
_____

Region
_____

Grape(s)
_____

Price   Product Code
_____

Appearance   Bouquet
_____

Taste   Body & Balance
_____

Comments
_____

GRAND RIDGE

Cabernet Sauvignon

2008

_____

CALIFORNIA
CANYON VINEYARDS

Paste your label here

Date Tasted

Wine

Occasion

Food Eaten with Wine

Other Guests

Producer/Vintner

Vintage

Region

Grape(s)

Price   Product Code

Appearance   Bouquet

Taste   Body & Balance

Comments

GRAND RIDGE

Cabernet Sauvignon

2008

CALIFORNIA
CANYON VINEYARDS

Paste your label here

102

Date Tasted
_____

Wine
_____

Occasion
_____

Food Eaten with Wine
_____

Other Guests
_____

Producer/Vintner
_____

Vintage
_____

Region
_____

Grape(s)
_____

Price   Product Code
_____

Appearance   Bouquet
_____

Taste   Body & Balance
_____

Comments
_____

GRAND RIDGE

Cabernet Sauvignon

2008

CALIFORNIA
CANYON VINEYARDS

Paste your label here

Tasting Notes | The Wine Lover's Journal

Date Tasted

Wine

Occasion

Food Eaten with Wine

Other Guests

Producer/Vintner

Vintage

Region

Grape(s)

Price   Product Code

Appearance   Bouquet

Taste   Body & Balance

Comments

GRAND RIDGE

∽

Cabernet Sauvignon

2008

CALIFORNIA
CANYON VINEYARDS

Paste your label here

Date Tasted

Wine

Occasion

Food Eaten with Wine

Other Guests

Producer/Vintner

Vintage

Region

Grape(s)

Price	Product Code
Appearance	Bouquet
Taste	Body & Balance

Comments

GRAND RIDGE

Cabernet Sauvignon

2008

CALIFORNIA
CANYON VINEYARDS

Paste your label here

Date Tasted

Wine

Occasion

Food Eaten with Wine

Other Guests

Producer/Vintner

Vintage

Region

Grape(s)

Price   Product Code

Appearance   Bouquet

Taste   Body & Balance

Comments

GRAND RIDGE

Cabernet Sauvignon

2008

CALIFORNIA
CANYON VINEYARDS

Paste your label here

Date Tasted
_____

Wine
_____

Occasion
_____

Food Eaten with Wine
_____

Other Guests
_____

Producer/Vintner
_____

Vintage
_____

Region
_____

Grape(s)
_____

Price   Product Code
_____

Appearance   Bouquet
_____

Taste   Body & Balance
_____

Comments
_____

GRAND RIDGE

Cabernet Sauvignon

2008
_____

CALIFORNIA
CANYON VINEYARDS

Paste your label here

Date Tasted
_____

Wine
_____

Occasion
_____

Food Eaten with Wine
_____

Other Guests
_____

Producer/Vintner
_____

Vintage
_____

Region
_____

Grape(s)
_____

Price   Product Code
_____

Appearance   Bouquet
_____

Taste   Body & Balance
_____

Comments
_____

GRAND RIDGE

Cabernet Sauvignon

2008

CALIFORNIA
CANYON VINEYARDS

Paste your label here

Date Tasted

Wine

Occasion

Food Eaten with Wine

Other Guests

Producer/Vintner

Vintage

Region

Grape(s)

Price   Product Code

Appearance   Bouquet

Taste   Body & Balance

Comments

GRAND RIDGE

∽

Cabernet Sauvignon

2008

CALIFORNIA
CANYON VINEYARDS

Paste your label here

Date Tasted
_____

Wine
_____

Occasion
_____

Food Eaten with Wine
_____

Other Guests
_____

Producer/Vintner
_____

Vintage
_____

Region
_____

Grape(s)
_____

Price   Product Code
_____

Appearance   Bouquet
_____

Taste   Body & Balance
_____

Comments
_____

GRAND RIDGE

∞

Cabernet Sauvignon

2008

CALIFORNIA
CANYON VINEYARDS

Paste your label here

Date Tasted
_____

Wine
_____

Occasion
_____

Food Eaten with Wine
_____

Other Guests
_____

Producer/Vintner
_____

Vintage
_____

Region
_____

Grape(s)
_____

Price   Product Code
_____

Appearance   Bouquet
_____

Taste   Body & Balance
_____

Comments
_____

GRAND RIDGE

Cabernet Sauvignon

2008

CALIFORNIA
CANYON VINEYARDS

Paste your label here

Tasting Notes | The Wine Lover's Journal

Date Tasted

Wine

Occasion

Food Eaten with Wine

Other Guests

Producer/Vintner

Vintage

Region

Grape(s)

Price   Product Code

Appearance   Bouquet

Taste   Body & Balance

Comments

GRAND RIDGE

Cabernet Sauvignon

2008

CALIFORNIA
CANYON VINEYARDS

Paste your label here

Date Tasted
_____

Wine
_____

Occasion
_____

Food Eaten with Wine
_____

Other Guests
_____

Producer/Vintner
_____

Vintage
_____

Region
_____

Grape(s)
_____

Price   Product Code
_____

Appearance   Bouquet
_____

Taste   Body & Balance
_____

Comments
_____

GRAND RIDGE

Cabernet Sauvignon

2008

CALIFORNIA
CANYON VINEYARDS

Paste your label here

Date Tasted

Wine

Occasion

Food Eaten with Wine

Other Guests

Producer/Vintner

Vintage

Region

Grape(s)

Price	Product Code
Appearance	Bouquet
Taste	Body & Balance

Comments

GRAND RIDGE

Cabernet Sauvignon

2008

CALIFORNIA
CANYON VINEYARDS

Paste your label here

Date Tasted

Wine

Occasion

Food Eaten with Wine

Other Guests

Producer/Vintner

Vintage

Region

Grape(s)

Price   Product Code

Appearance   Bouquet

Taste   Body & Balance

Comments

GRAND RIDGE

Cabernet Sauvignon

2008

CALIFORNIA
CANYON VINEYARDS

Paste your label here

Date Tasted
_____

Wine
_____

Occasion
_____

Food Eaten with Wine
_____

Other Guests
_____

Producer/Vintner
_____

Vintage
_____

Region
_____

Grape(s)
_____

Price _____ Product Code

Appearance _____ Bouquet

Taste _____ Body & Balance

Comments
_____

GRAND RIDGE

Cabernet Sauvignon

2008

CALIFORNIA
CANYON VINEYARDS

Paste your label here

Date Tasted

Wine

Occasion

Food Eaten with Wine

Other Guests

Producer/Vintner

Vintage

Region

Grape(s)

Price   Product Code

Appearance   Bouquet

Taste   Body & Balance

Comments

GRAND RIDGE

Cabernet Sauvignon

2008

CALIFORNIA
CANYON VINEYARDS

Paste your label here

Date Tasted

Wine

Occasion

Food Eaten with Wine

Other Guests

Producer/Vintner

Vintage

Region

Grape(s)

Price   Product Code

Appearance   Bouquet

Taste   Body & Balance

Comments

GRAND RIDGE

Cabernet Sauvignon

2008

CALIFORNIA
CANYON VINEYARDS

Paste your label here

Date Tasted

Wine

Occasion

Food Eaten with Wine

Other Guests

Producer/Vintner

Vintage

Region

Grape(s)

Price   Product Code

Appearance   Bouquet

Taste   Body & Balance

Comments

GRAND RIDGE

Cabernet Sauvignon

2008

CALIFORNIA
CANYON VINEYARDS

Paste your label here

Date Tasted

Wine

Occasion

Food Eaten with Wine

Other Guests

Producer/Vintner

Vintage

Region

Grape(s)

Price	Product Code
Appearance	Bouquet
Taste	Body & Balance

Comments

GRAND RIDGE

Cabernet Sauvignon

2008

CALIFORNIA
CANYON VINEYARDS

Paste your label here

Date Tasted

Wine

Occasion

Food Eaten with Wine

Other Guests

Producer/Vintner

Vintage

Region

Grape(s)

Price   Product Code

Appearance   Bouquet

Taste   Body & Balance

Comments

GRAND RIDGE

Cabernet Sauvignon

2008

CALIFORNIA
CANYON VINEYARDS

Paste your label here

Date Tasted

Wine

Occasion

Food Eaten with Wine

Other Guests

Producer/Vintner

Vintage

Region

Grape(s)

Price   Product Code

Appearance   Bouquet

Taste   Body & Balance

Comments

GRAND RIDGE

Cabernet Sauvignon

2008

CALIFORNIA
CANYON VINEYARDS

Paste your label here

Date Tasted

Wine

Occasion

Food Eaten with Wine

Other Guests

Producer/Vintner

Vintage

Region

Grape(s)

Price   Product Code

Appearance   Bouquet

Taste   Body & Balance

Comments

GRAND RIDGE

Cabernet Sauvignon

2008

CALIFORNIA
CANYON VINEYARDS

Paste your label here

Date Tasted

Wine

Occasion

Food Eaten with Wine

Other Guests

Producer/Vintner

Vintage

Region

Grape(s)

Price   Product Code

Appearance   Bouquet

Taste   Body & Balance

Comments

GRAND RIDGE

Cabernet Sauvignon

2008

CALIFORNIA
CANYON VINEYARDS

Paste your label here

Date Tasted

Wine

Occasion

Food Eaten with Wine

Other Guests

Producer/Vintner

Vintage

Region

Grape(s)

Price	Product Code
Appearance	Bouquet
Taste	Body & Balance

Comments

GRAND RIDGE

Cabernet Sauvignon

2008

CALIFORNIA
CANYON VINEYARDS

Paste your label here

Date Tasted

Wine

Occasion

Food Eaten with Wine

Other Guests

Producer/Vintner

Vintage

Region

Grape(s)

Price   Product Code

Appearance   Bouquet

Taste   Body & Balance

Comments

GRAND RIDGE

Cabernet Sauvignon

2008

CALIFORNIA
CANYON VINEYARDS

Paste your label here

Notes

Notes

Third edition 2008

For additional information, please contact Whitecap Books, 351 Lynn Avenue, North Vancouver, BC V7J 2C4. Visit our website at www.whitecap.ca.

Edited by Ben D'Andrea
Typesetting by Marjolein Visser and Claire Leila Philipson
Wine labels by Michelle Mayne
Additional image editing by Five Seventeen

Printed and bound in China

Library and Archives Canada Cataloguing in Publication

Rundall, Clare.
A wine lover's journal

ISBN 1-55285-941-X
ISBN 978-1-55285-941-4

1. Wine and wine making—Miscellanea. 2. Wine tasting—Miscellanea. I. Moore, John. II. Title.
TP548.R86 2003   641.2'2   C2003-910238-6

The publisher acknowledges the financial support of the Government of Canada through the Book Publishing Industry Development Program (BPIDP) for our publishing activities and the province of British Columbia through the Book Publishing Tax Credit.